SAMURAI

The Story of a Warrior

Dee Phillips

READZONE

READZONE

First published in this edition 2014

The right of the Author to be identified as the Author of this work has been asserted by the Author in accordance with the Copyright, Designs and Patents Act 1988

Every attempt has been made by the Publisher to secure appropriate permissions for material reproduced in this book. If there has been any oversight we will be happy to rectify the situation in future editions or reprints. Written submissions should be made to the Publishers.

British Library Cataloguing in Publication Data (CIP) is available for this title.

ISBN 978-1-78322-518-7

Printed in Malta by Melita Press

Developed and Created by Ruby Tuesday Books Ltd
Project Director – Ruth Owen
Designer – Elaine Wilkinson

Images courtesy of Corbis (page 43), Getty Images (pages 14–15t, 24tl), Istock, Shutterstock and Superstock (cover, pages 3, 7, 9c, 12t, 15tr, 19, 23r, 26br, 31br, 33, 35c, 40, 45tr).

Acknowledgements
With thanks to Lorraine Petersen, Educational Consultant, for her help in the development and creation of these books

Visit our website: www.readzonebooks.com

We face each other on the battlefield.

Two proud samurai.

Revenge burns in my heart.

Here is where it ends.

SAMURAI

The Story of a Warrior

In medieval times, Japan was ruled by mighty warlords.

They fought each other for land.

They went to war to win power.

Every warlord gathered around him an army of warriors.

These fearsome fighters were trained from childhood.

They were skilful and brutal.

They had no fear of death.

They were the

SAMURAI

Those Who Serve

We face each other on the battlefield.
Two proud samurai.

My body aches from fighting.
My armour is thick with blood.

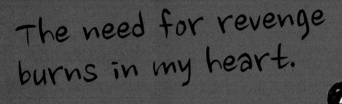

The need for revenge
burns in my heart.

We face each other on
the battlefield.
Two proud samurai.

The battle rages around us.
No other man will join our
fight, though.
That is not the samurai way.

Revenge burns in my heart.

Here is where
        it ends.

I was born the son of a samurai.

My father was our lord's
most loyal warrior.

I was born in our lord's castle.

I often watched my father
ride off to battle.

One day, I would be a samurai, too.

Our lord had enemies.
My father rode off to battle
many times.
He fought bravely.
He killed many enemy samurai.

My father served our
lord well.

It was the summer of my ninth year.
An army marched on the castle.
There were thousands of
enemy samurai.

From high on the castle wall,
I watched the battle.
I watched my father kill
many men.

Finally, the army's general
stood before him.

I watched my father face
the general.
Two proud samurai.
No other man would join
their fight.

Their swords clashed.
My father fought bravely.
He fought until the final blow.

From high on the castle wall,
I watched.

I watched as my father's
head rolled in the dust.

I watched the enemy general lift
up my father's head.
He rode from the battlefield.
His prize hung by his side.

All that was left in the dust
was my father's blood.

The battle raged on.

When night came, we escaped.
Our lord and his bodyguards.
My mother and I.
We escaped to a castle in the mountains.

I left behind the place where I was born.
I left behind my father's blood in the dust.

The need for revenge burned in my heart.

And so it began.

I studied hard.
I trained hard, too.
My body ached from fighting.

My wooden sword was a
brutal weapon.

I did not see the boys that faced me.
I saw only the enemy general.

The samurai who left my father's
blood in the dust.

The years passed.

I could ride faster than
any other boy.
My arrows flew straight
to their targets.
In my hands, a spear was
a brutal weapon.

The years passed.

For me there was nothing else.

I slept so I could be faster.
I ate so I would grow stronger.

My horse.
My bow.
My spear and my sword.

The need for revenge burned
in my heart.

For me there was nothing else.

One day my teacher said, "You are ready."
He handed me a sword.

"This was your father's sword," he said.
"It took many heads. It will do so again."

I held the sword in my hands.
I did not see the battles that faced me.
I saw only the enemy general.

The samurai who left my father's blood in the dust.

Now I was a samurai warrior.
When my lord rode off to battle,
I went too.
My sword took many heads.
I was not afraid of death.

By day I was a warrior.
But at night in my dreams, I was a
small boy.
A small boy high on a castle wall.

A small boy with revenge in his heart.

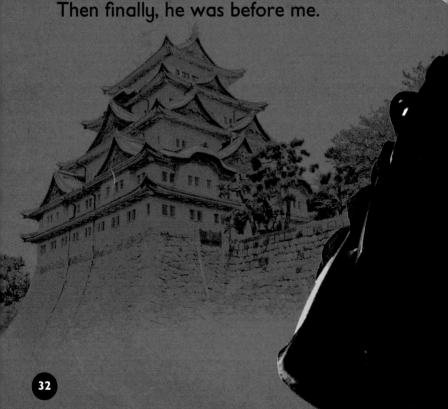

Now I stand proud on a battlefield.

We marched on a castle.
The castle where I was born.
The castle they took from us all
those years ago.

The enemy samurai faced us.
I fought bravely.
My armour was thick with blood.

Then finally, he was before me.

We face each other on
the battlefield.
Two proud samurai.

The battle rages around us.
No other man will join our
fight, though.
That is not the samurai way.

Revenge burns in my heart.

Here is where
            it ends.

Our swords clash.
We slash.
We thrust.
Again and again.

He fights bravely.
He fights until the final blow.

The enemy general falls to his knees.
My sword slices through the air.

I watch his head
roll in the dust.

I lift up the general's head.
I leave only blood in the dust.
I have my revenge.

It is ended.

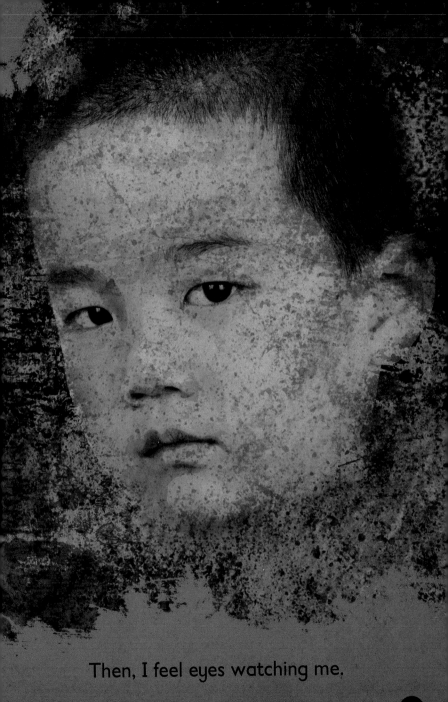

Then, I feel eyes watching me.

High on the castle wall, I see a young boy.
He is watching the battle.
He watches as I ride away.
My prize hung at my side.

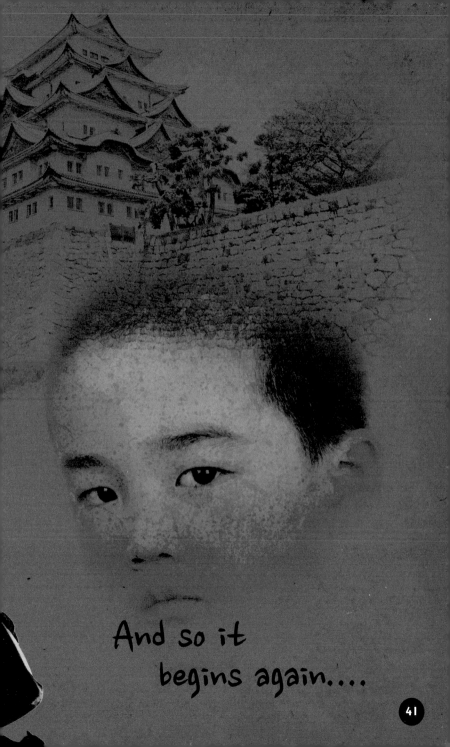

And so it
begins again....

SAMURAI:

Behind the Story

There were samurai in Japan from around the year AD 800 to the late 1800s.

Japan was led by an emperor, but he had no real power. It was the warlords, or *daimyos*, who truly controlled Japan. One warlord was made *shogun*, and he ruled alongside the emperor. From around AD 1000 until 1600, Japan's warlords fought each other to gain land and power. From around 1600 onward, the warring families tried to unite.

To become a samurai warrior, you had to be born to a samurai family. Samurai boys trained in horse-riding, archery and spear fighting. Swordfighting was taught by a teacher called a *sensei*. Samurai swords were too dangerous to use in training. So samurai practised using wooden copies.

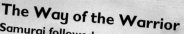

The Way of the Warrior

Samurai followed a code called *Bushido*, or "The Way of the Warrior". These rules set out how a samurai should live.

- A samurai should be loyal to his lord and follow his every order.
- A samurai should be fearless and willing to die for his lord.
- A samurai must have great self-control. He should not cheat or show off.

By his early twenties, a samurai was ready to serve his lord. A samurai warrior had no fear of death. To die in battle was honourable.

A samurai fought with a long sword called a *katana* and a short sword called a *wakizashi*. It was said that a *katana*'s blade could cut through a pile of seven dead bodies in a single swipe!

katana sword

wakizashi sword

SAMURAI – What's next?

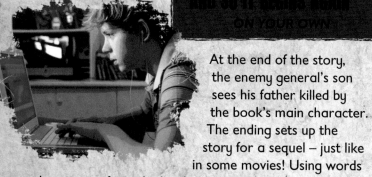

AND SO IT BEGINS AGAIN
ON YOUR OWN

At the end of the story, the enemy general's son sees his father killed by the book's main character. The ending sets up the story for a sequel – just like in some movies! Using words and sentences from the book, write a sequel. Imagine you are the enemy general's son.

• How do you get your revenge?

THE WAY OF THE WARRIOR
ON YOUR OWN, WITH A PARTNER, IN A GROUP

Samurai lived by a code, or set of rules (see page 43). What rules do you think people should try to live by in our modern world? How would these rules make life better?

Try writing a code for life in the 21st century.

Samurai lived hundreds of years ago. Their world was very different to our modern world. Do you think the kind of loyalty they showed to their lords still exists? Discuss the ways in which people might show extreme loyalty today.

- In what ways might loyalty help a person or group?

- Are there times, however, when loyalty without question can be a bad thing?

BE A SCRIPT WRITER
ON YOUR OWN / WITH A PARTNER / IN A GROUP

Samurai have featured in many action movies. Try being a script writer for a samurai movie. Choose a scene from the book. In your script, describe the setting for the scene. What do the actors wear? What kind of make-up will they need? Will there be special effects in the scene? Write the dialogue, or words, for the actors to speak. Then try acting out the scene with friends!

45

Titles in the
Yesterday's Voices
series

VIKING
The Story of a Raider
Dee Phillips

We jump from our
ship and attack. But
something feels wrong.
I know this place….

SAMURAI
The Story of a Warrior
Dee Phillips

We face each other.
Two proud samurai.
Revenge burns in
my heart.

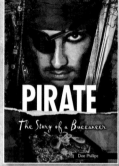

PIRATE
The Story of a Buccaneer
Dee Phillips

We saw a treasure
ship. Up went our
black flag. They could
not escape….

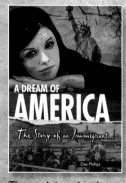

A DREAM OF
AMERICA
The Story of an Immigrant
Dee Phillips

The work is so hard.
I miss my home. Will
my dream of America
come true?

RESISTANCE
FIGHTER
The Story of a Secret War
Dee Phillips

I jumped from the plane.
I carried fake papers, a
gun and a radio. Now I
was Sylvie, a resistance
fighter….

VIETNAM
The Story of a Marine
Dee Phillips

Every day we went on
patrol. The Viet Cong hid
in jungles and villages.
We had to find them,
before they found us.